T0009917

MINDFULNESS FOR

FALLING ASLEEP

PRISCILLA AN

childsworld.com

The
**Child's
World**
childsworld.com

Published by The Child's World
800-599-READ · www.childsworld.com

Photography Credits
Photographs ©: Kleber Cordeiro/Shutterstock Images,
cover, 1, 15, 16–17, 19, 20; Stanislav Samoylik/Shutterstock
Images, 3; Shutterstock Images, 4–5, 12–13; Prostock
Studio/Shutterstock Images, 7, 8, 10–11; VIS Fine Art/
Shutterstock Images, 22

ISBN Information
9781503869660 (Reinforced Library Binding)
9781503880870 (Portable Document Format)
9781503882188 (Online Multi-user eBook)
9781503883499 (Electronic Publication)
9781645498629 (Paperback)

LCCN 2022951167

Printed in the United States of America

Priscilla An is a children's book
editor and author. She lives in
Minnesota with her rabbit and
likes to practice mindfulness
through yoga.

TABLE OF CONTENTS

CHAPTER 1

WHAT IS MINDFULNESS?

Falling asleep can be hard. Sometimes, people want to stay awake to do things that seem more fun than sleeping. Other times, feeling scared or nervous can keep people awake. Practicing mindfulness can help with falling asleep. Mindfulness is when people notice their thoughts, feelings, and surroundings. Being mindful can help people relax. It can help people think positively. Feeling relaxed and positive can make a person feel safe. This can make it easier to sleep.

Sleeping helps the body rest. It gives people energy for the day.

MINDFULNESS MEDITATION

Maya is playing dress-up with her dad. They are pretending they are princesses. Maya's dad even lets her paint his nails! She is having a lot of fun.

Maya looks at the clock on the wall. It says it is 8:30 p.m. That means it is her bedtime. But Maya does not want to go to sleep. Sleep feels like a waste of time. Maya wants to keep playing!

Sometimes people do not want to sleep when they are having fun.

SLEEP IS IMPORTANT

People need sleep to survive. Having enough sleep can make people feel less cranky and tired. Getting enough sleep can help the body fight off sickness. Sleep can even help kids grow.

Listening to bedtime stories can be relaxing.

"Maya," her dad says. "It's time for bed." He takes the crowns from their heads and puts them away.

"No," Maya groans. "Can we play for just ten more minutes?"

Her dad shakes his head. "Princesses need their rest! How about I read you a bedtime story?"

"Fine," Maya says. Her dad makes the best voices when he reads!

Maya's dad takes out her favorite book. It is about a monkey named Rocky who lives in a rain forest. Rocky has many friends, including a tiger and a frog. After her dad finishes the story, Maya still feels wide awake.

Sometimes people have a hard time falling asleep.

"I wonder what it would be like to be a monkey," Maya giggles. "I wouldn't need to go to school!" She wiggles around in her bed.

Maya's dad smiles at her. "But if you were a monkey, I would miss you a lot!" He kisses her forehead. "Maybe you can pretend you're a monkey. Close your eyes. We can try doing a **meditation** to help you sleep."

Maya closes her eyes. She **focuses** on her dad's **soothing** voice.

"Take a deep breath," he says. "Breathe out slowly, like you are blowing a really big bubble." He pauses and waits for Maya breathe out. "Do it one more time. Try to keep breathing like this while I'm talking."

"Now imagine that you are a monkey," Maya's dad says. "You are hanging backward on a tree branch. Your tail is holding you up. You see the colorful red and yellow flowers in the rain forest. You hear parrots chirping and frogs croaking. The wind blows through your fur. It feels soft, like a blanket. The warm sun is in your eyes. You blink slowly. Your body feels tired. You want to sleep on your branch."

As he talks, Maya imagines herself as a monkey. She continues breathing deeply. Slowly, Maya drifts off to sleep. When Maya wakes up the next morning, she feels **refreshed**. She is ready to take on the new day.

Sometimes focusing on something specific, such as imagining life as a monkey, can make meditation easier.

CHAPTER 3

ALLEN THE HERO

Luka's parents are gone for the night. His babysitter says he can watch one movie before going to sleep. Luka is excited! He picks a movie his friends told him about. But it is scarier than he expects. There are ghosts and monsters.

Watching a scary movie before bedtime may make it more difficult to fall asleep.

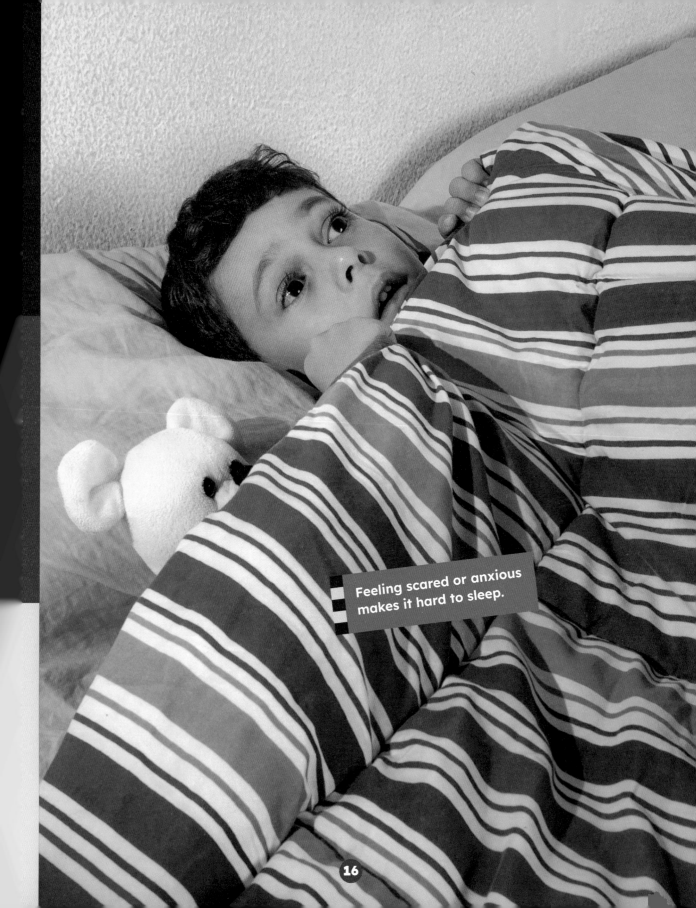

Feeling scared or anxious makes it hard to sleep.

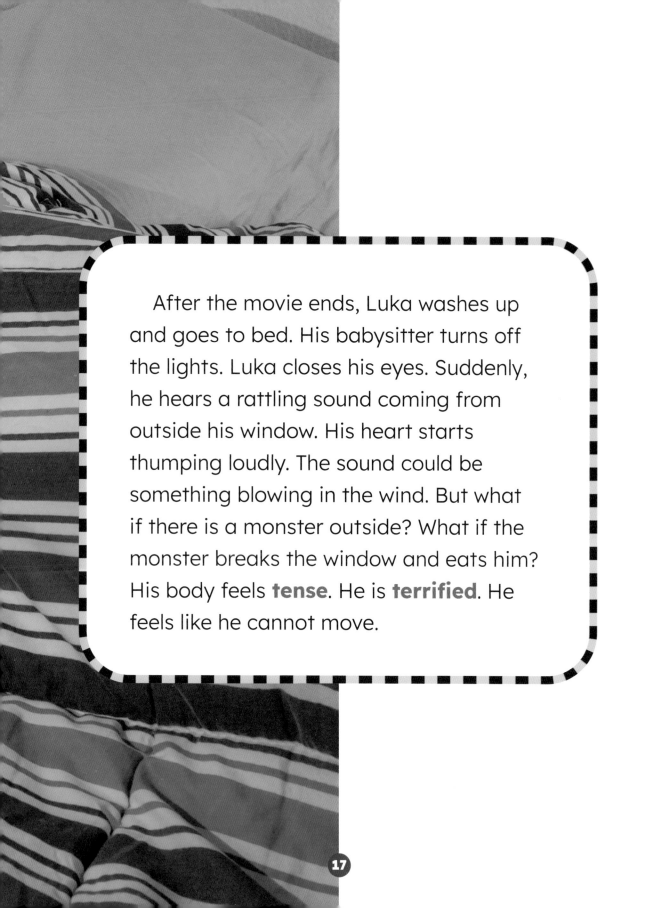

After the movie ends, Luka washes up and goes to bed. His babysitter turns off the lights. Luka closes his eyes. Suddenly, he hears a rattling sound coming from outside his window. His heart starts thumping loudly. The sound could be something blowing in the wind. But what if there is a monster outside? What if the monster breaks the window and eats him? His body feels **tense**. He is **terrified**. He feels like he cannot move.

Luka thinks about the movie he watched. There were ghosts and monsters, but there were also heroes who defeated them. Luka looks at Allen, his teddy bear. He pulls Allen close to his chest. He squeezes his eyes shut. He imagines that Allen becomes really big. The bear lifts Luka on top of his fluffy shoulders. Allen opens a magic door. He takes Luka to a different world where teddy bears are heroes and fight monsters.

As Luka uses his imagination, his fear slowly goes away. He forgets about the sound outside his window. His body relaxes into his bed. His muscles are no longer tense. Now they feel soft.

Keeping a stuffed animal nearby may help people feel safe enough to fall asleep.

IMAGINATION
Imagination is one of the mind's most powerful tools. It is also important when practicing mindfulness. Imagination can help people focus on positive experiences and emotions. It can also help people relax.

Getting plenty of sleep is important.

Luka's heartbeat slows down. His eyes flutter, and soon he is fast asleep.

The next morning, Luka's mom wakes him up for breakfast. "Did you sleep well?" she asks. Luka nods happily. He tells her that Allen helped him fall asleep.

At first, Luka's whole body felt like it was being controlled by fear. But using his imagination helped Luka take control of his thoughts. It also helped calm his body and his mind.

WONDER MORE

Wondering about New Information

How much did you know about mindfulness and sleep before reading this book? What new information did you learn? Write down two new facts that this book taught you. Was the new information surprising? Why or why not?

Wondering How It Matters

What is one way practicing mindfulness to fall asleep relates to your life? How do you think it relates to other kids' lives?

Wondering Why

Mindful meditation can help people fall asleep. Why do you think it is important to get plenty of sleep? Do you think using mindful meditation before bed could help you?

Ways to Keep Wondering

Mindfulness can be a complex topic. After reading this book, what questions do you have about it? What can you do to learn more about mindfulness?

ANIMAL BREATHING EXERCISE

Try this breathing exercise to help you relax before going to sleep.

1. Go through your bedtime routine. Once you are ready to sleep, turn off the lights and get into a comfortable position in your bed.

2. Close your eyes and focus on breathing slowly. Notice the way your belly moves as you breathe in and out.

3. When you breathe out, imagine that you are an animal. You can choose to be a busy bee and make a *bzzz* sound. You can try being a cat and make a purring sound.

4. As you breathe, feel your body relax and sink into your bed. Before you know it, you might be fast asleep!

GLOSSARY

focuses (FOH-kuss-iz) When someone focuses, she pays special attention to something. Maya focuses on her dad's voice to fall asleep.

meditation (meh-dih-TAY-shuhn) When someone does a meditation, she calms her body and thoughts. Maya's dad helped her fall asleep by doing a mindfulness meditation.

refreshed (reh-FRESHT) When a person feels refreshed, she feels strong and energized. Maya felt refreshed after waking up from a good night's sleep.

soothing (SOOTH-ing) When something is soothing, it feels calming and comforting. Maya's dad had a soothing voice.

tense (TENSS) Being tense means feeling stiff and tight. When Luka was scared, his body became tense.

terrified (TEH-rih-fyed) When someone feels terrified, he is very scared. Luka was terrified when he thought there might be a monster outside his window.

FIND OUT MORE

In the Library

An, Priscilla. *Mindfulness with Friends.*
Parker, CO: The Child's World, 2024.

Willard, Christopher, and Olivia Weisser. *The Breathing Book.* Boulder, CO: Sounds True, 2020.

Woodgate, Vicky. *The Magic of Sleep.*
New York, NY: DK Publishing, 2021.

On the Web

Visit our website for links about mindfulness for falling asleep:

childsworld.com/links

Note to Parents, Caregivers, Teachers, and Librarians: We routinely verify our Web links to make sure they are safe and active sites. So encourage your readers to check them out!

INDEX